Clairvoyance and Psychic Development

The complete guide to clairvoyance, psychic development, and using your psychic ability!

Copyright 2015

Table Of Contents

Introduction 1

Chapter 1: The Different Kinds of Psychic Abilities 2

Chapter 2: Important Pointers in Developing Psychic Skills 8

Chapter 3: Preparing Yourself for Psychic Functioning by Sharpening Your Senses 15

Chapter 4: Psychic Skill Training 18

Chapter 5: Honing Your Clairvoyance and Other Psychic Abilities 29

Conclusion 32

Introduction

I want to thank you and congratulate you for downloading the book, "Clairvoyance and Psychic Development".

This book contains helpful information about clairvoyance and other psychic abilities, what they are, and how they work!

You will learn about clairvoyance, divination, telepathy, telekinesis, and many other psychic abilities. You'll also be given steps to develop each of the psychic abilities in yourself.

Through reading this book, you'll be able to get more in tune with your psychic abilities, and better understand the psychic world around you.

This book will explain to you tips and techniques that will allow you to successfully understand and begin using your psychic abilities to better enhance your life.

Developing your psychic abilities is fun and rewarding, read on to learn how you can begin!

Thanks again for downloading this book, I hope you enjoy it!

Chapter 1:
The Different Kinds of Psychic Abilities

Extra-sensory Perception (ESP) is the ability to perceive things beyond the normal range of the human senses. ESP is closely related to psychic abilities, which are skills that are currently inexplicable by science. The term psychic comes from the word psyche or mind/soul. It is theorized that these powers come from the soul itself because they don't follow natural laws.

There are many kinds of psychic abilities:

- Clairvoyance – Acquiring psychic information through the sense of sight (not necessarily through the eyes, but the information comes in a visual form)

- Clairaudience – Gathering psychic information through hearing. This may be heard as if it was an actual sound or you may hear some words or tunes in your head.

- Clairsentience – Receiving psychic information through the sense of touch. It's feeling something that wasn't caused by a person or an object.

- Clairalience – Getting psychic information in the form of smells. This smell doesn't emanate from something in the immediate environment, but may be symbolic or a message from other beings.

- Clairgustance – Tasting psychic information. Again, the taste is not caused by something that is recently eaten but it comes out of seemingly nowhere.

- Claircognizance – Attaining knowledge of a subject through extraordinary means (not through the 5 senses). This is sometimes called as direct knowing or intuition.

- Precognition – Knowing what will happen and what a person will do in the future.

- Retrocognition – Same as precognition but the focus is on the past.

- Psychometry – Deriving information by touching an object. The information may take any form – visual, auditory, tactile, etc.

- Psychic Dreams – Getting information or interacting with others through dreams. This is similar to lucid dreaming (dreaming while awake), veridical dreams (dreams that turn out to be true), and prophetic dreams (dreams that foretell the future).

- Telepathy – The ability to transfer and receive thoughts to and from others, not only humans but other living beings as well. This is different from cold reading or reading a person through his/her mannerisms, appearance, and conversations. Telepathy is direct mind-to-mind communication and it doesn't depend on outside cues. Animal communicators practice a form of telepathy with creatures.

- Empathy – Same as telepathy but on the emotional level. This is different from reading body language and knowing what a person feels through it. Empathy is feeling the person or animal's emotions as if they were your own, and you don't rely on your ordinary senses to do it.

- Telekinesis – The ability to move objects and energy through the mind and not using any physical force or tool. There are many kinds of telekinesis such as pyrokinesis (control of fire), electrokinesis (control of electricity), and so on. Some people are born with this skill but others can also achieve it with intense practice.

- Psychic Healing – The ability to heal and cure illnesses through extraordinary ways. Reiki, pranic healing, crystal healing, and visualizations are some forms of psychic healing.

Interested in the skills mentioned above? You will learn how to do each one of them in a moment. But first, let's discuss clairvoyance more deeply.

Among all the psychic powers, clairvoyance is the skill that is most commonly linked to psychic abilities. In fact, the third-eye chakra, or the energy center associated with the psychic side of man, implies that psychic sensing is mostly visual. This is somewhat true since the dominant sense in most people is the sight. However, psychic information can be obtained through all the senses, and sometimes a person just knows something even though he or she can't point out why.

The following paranormal activities are a subset of clairvoyance:

Seeing Auras

The aura is the energy field of a person. It is said to be the product of the energy centers (chakras) that line a person's spine. Seeing the aura provides more than entertainment because it also gives a lot of clues about the person, such as his/her state of physical and psychological health, current emotions, past history, and so on.

Seeing Invisible Beings and Energies

The things that humans see are limited to the visual spectrum of light. Everything beyond that is only seen with the help of instruments, which translate the energies into something we can perceive and understand. This is enough to tell us that what we perceive through our eyes is not all that there is. Our myths and legends are filled with stories about fantastic creatures. We hear about psychics seeing things that a normal person could not. Sometimes, a sane person who doesn't consider himself a psychic can see ghosts, fairies, and outlandish creatures which they have never seen before. All of these tales and narratives point to a bigger reality than what our 5 senses present to us. Being clairvoyant extends the scope of vision so that we can see more of the universe.

Interacting with the Unseen

It's best if you develop your clairvoyant abilities if you want to be in tune with the realm of spirits and energies. Spirit communication, energy manipulation, spell creation, and similar activities are largely dependent on the capability to see beyond what is normally seen. Of course, sending healing energies or talking with ghosts is doable even if you don't see what you're dealing with, but it's better if you do. If you're clairvoyant, you will know whether you are talking with the right spirit or an impostor, and you will know the effects of the projected energies upon the body of the person you're healing.

Crystal Gazing

Crystal gazing is an ancient art of using a crystal to view the hidden world. Crystal gazers see many things in their tool, such as clouds, colors, and even detailed visions. There are books that prescribe ways on how to interpret the things that are seen. However, you don't have to rely on other people's interpretations because you will be using your own psychic mind. Just the same, this book includes the traditional interpretations and instructions on how to decipher them using your own methods.

Remote Viewing

Remote viewing is seeing things that are hidden or at a distance from the viewer. Interestingly, remote viewing was studied by the governments of the USA, UK, and Russia because they realized the immense value of this information-gathering skill. With remote viewing, you can find missing persons and objects, know whether a person is still alive or not, know the characteristics of a subject even though it's far from your reach at the moment, map a place of interest, spot any dangers in a location, know what people are up to, and more. You will also learn how to do remote viewing from this book.

Divination

Divination is the practice of knowing the future or the unknown through tools and techniques. Some examples of divination tools are Tarot cards, the I-Ching, astrology, numerology, geomancy, runes, and crystal gazing. Although these tools are a great help for divination, you can divine without them. This book will teach you how to do both tool-based divination and freehand divination.

Seeing Visions

Visions can be about anything: the future, the answer to your question, an insight to a person or topic, a perception of the normally invisible, etc. You can see visions within your mind or out there with your physical eyes. You will learn how to do both mental and visual perception so that you will have greater flexibility in exercising clairvoyance.

The things mentioned above are not the only things that you can do with clairvoyance. You will find other applications for them as the days go by and you get used to practicing your psychic abilities. For example, you can use your clairvoyance to know whether a person is trustworthy or not, or know whether a particular store is open or closed at the moment. You can also use your gift of vision to nurture your creativity, or get some ideas for solving a particular problem.

Whenever you think about an application for clairvoyance or any other psychic ability, write it down. Doing so informs the psychic aspect of your mind that you are serious in developing its talents. Also, if you get ideas on how to use it out of the blue, it might be a sign that your psychic mind is trying to help you out. Welcome these insights and act upon them if it's safe and productive to do so.

Chapter 2:
Important Pointers in Developing Psychic Skills

There are some things you have to keep in mind if you intend to develop clairvoyance and the other psychic gifts:

- Reaching the psychic state of mind

- Distinguishing genuine psychic information from other things like imagination, fears, expectations, and projections

- Interpreting the psychic impressions

- Making your psychic abilities work reliably

Reaching your psychic level

As you may have guessed by reading the previous paragraphs, your psychic mind is different from your normal mind. You have both kinds of minds; everyone does. Each individual has the potential to become psychic if he or she knows how to alter his or her state of consciousness. Scientifically speaking, the brain produces different kinds of brainwaves:

Beta (12 to 25 cycles per second) – the level of ordinary consciousness and what we use as we go about our daily routines. It is active when we use logic and reasoning.

Alpha (6 to 14 cycles per second) – relaxed awareness where daydreams and dreams during sleep occur. This is the level that allows people to have some psychic experiences.

Theta (4 to 8 cycles per second) – this is a state of deep trance and sleep. Most psychic skills are manifested with this level, especially difficult feats like telekinesis.

Delta (less than 4 cycles per second) – a person is fully unconscious during the delta state.

As mentioned before, psychic abilities don't follow natural laws. In simpler words, science still doesn't understand why they work and why they are more commonly exhibited during certain brainwave states. However, other fields of knowledge such as parapsychology (the study of paranormal mental phenomena) and quantum physics (the study of subatomic particles) offer some guesses. One interesting theory is that everything and everyone in the Universe is linked to each other via energy strings; thus, it's possible to derive information from other objects/creatures and to influence them without physical means. The high frequencies of Beta create a mental barrier that makes a person focus only on a narrow scope of his/her existence. By moving away from this mental state, it may be possible to reopen the connections between the person's mind and the rest of creation – such as with telekinetics who can move objects without touching them, or with psychics who can read people's life histories just by looking at them.

A person goes through all four cycles (Beta, Alpha, Theta, and Delta) during his/her waking and sleeping hours and the periods in between them (hypnagogia). However, the regular person doesn't usually pay attention when he or she is in other states aside from the Beta state. As a result, he/she goes through the psychic levels of Alpha and Theta without willfully benefitting from them. Although spontaneous psychic information may come regardless of the person's state of mind at the moment, it's better to know how to achieve these states at will to gain control of the process.

So, here are some things you need to practice:

- Going to Alpha and Theta at will
- Remain in that level for as long as you need to

How to Lower Your Brainwaves

Brainwaves are raised by the following things: stimuli, thought, and some substances like coffee and alertness-inducing medication. To make your brainwaves slow down, you need to stay away from things that speed them up. That means reducing distractions – external stimuli such as lights and noise, and internal stimuli like worries and ruminations. Avoid drinking coffee or doing anything else that will make you jittery and uncomfortable.

Nothing is more important in psychic training than lowering your brainwaves, and one way to do this is through relaxing your mind and body. You can also close your eyes with the intention of going deeper into your mind – it was found out that closing the eyes can help the production of Alpha and Theta brainwaves because 1: The brain regions responsible for automatic body processes think that the person is about to sleep and 2: Visual stimuli are blocked, thus distractions are greatly reduced. Visualization also helps because the subconscious mind (the part of the mind in tune with psychic skills) responds to visualized scenes.

Relaxation

If you have a particular ritual for getting relaxed, you can use that for achieving a psychic state. Otherwise, find something relaxing to do. This can be as complicated as performing a yoga routine or as simple as sitting and closing your eyes. One method you can do is to gradually relax your entire body. Focus on the crown of your head and will it to relax. Move on to your forehead and loosen any tightness in there. Continue doing this with each part until you are completely tension-free. You can also do this the other way around, starting from your toes and working your way up.

If a part of your body is uncomfortable and you can't do anything about it at the moment, you can either send healing energies to it or use the sensations to propel you deeper into the psychic level. Acknowledge the sensations, talk to the body part, thank it for informing you of its condition, and resolve to do something about it later (the body has an awareness of its own, so it's not entirely nonsensical to talk to it). Give an instruction to make the sensations fade away. Convert the feelings into something symbolic, such as an object with a color and shape, and imagine it growing smaller and dimmer until nothing remains – this technique is used by many people for pain control.

If you are okay with the unpleasant sensations, you can make the pain become a catalyst for your mind to switch into psychic mode. Tell yourself over and over again, "The pain/discomfort I am feeling is putting me deeper and deeper into a trance." Make everything you experience help you get to the psychic level.

Visualizations

Visualizations, or imagined visions, can be used to direct the mind. Visualizations are used for mental programming (you can learn more about this in hypnosis and law-of-attraction books) and lowering brain frequencies. You can create your own visualized scenes that symbolize your intention to slow down your brainwaves and become more psychic. Otherwise, you can do the following:

Imagine a relaxing scene – Pleasant scenery is calming; we humans are born with the tendency to like beautiful environments because we are dependent upon the surroundings to survive. When our territory is safe and nurturing, we tend feel good and relax. Also, we respond to imagined scenes as if they were real because we have brain parts that can't distinguish reality from imagination. Simply put, when we imagine being in a place that relaxes us, our brainwaves reflect that relaxation as well – which makes it easier to do psychic activities.

Imagine going down – The subconscious understands symbols more than it does words, so if you want to communicate with it and direct it, you need to use symbols instead of straightforward reasoning (reasoning is the expertise of the conscious mind, which is not that good with psychic phenomena). One easy way to symbolize going deeper is to pretend that you're going down a flight of stairs or a ladder. State that as you go down, you are entering more deeply into the psychic level.

Count backwards – Counting down provides a way to focus on something simple (important in staying conscious) while deepening your awareness. Again, you must have the intention of entering the psychic level so you increase your chances of reaching Alpha or Theta. Initially, start with higher numbers such as 300. Do this regularly until your mind gets used to reducing its level if you count backwards. There will come a time when you will be able to gain psychic awareness by counting from 10 to 1 or even just 3 to 1.

Other Ways to Reach Altered States

Controlling your breath. The way you breathe affects your mental state – if you breathe fast, your stress levels rise, and when you breathe slowly and fully, you become relaxed. Take deep breaths for a couple of minutes, with the intention of activating your psychic senses.

Vocalizing mantras. Mantras spoken repeatedly have the capability of putting a person into a light trance. You can also create a mantra of your own, such as "I am becoming more and more psychic" and other affirmations.

Focusing on a single object. Because overstimulation ruins sensitivity, you need to focus on a simple subject if you want to achieve a receptive state of mind. This focal point serves to keep you awake while you're winding down. You can fix your eyes on a particular item or meditate on one topic.

Listening to music. Music activates the entire brain so it can easily alter brainwaves. Choose music that relaxes you. There are some sound tracks that are made to specifically induce trance states. Shamanic drumming and binaural beats are some examples.

Listening to a guided meditation. You can find recordings of guided meditations in record shops and new age stores. They give instructions on what to do to relax yourself, and some deal specifically with psychic development.

Physical overexertion. Shamans and mystics sometimes subject themselves to excruciating ordeals such as fasting, spinning around wildly, inflicting pain upon themselves, and burying themselves partially in the ground for days. This makes their brain go into survival mode, thus they can no longer maintain Beta. You don't have to do these! You can be psychic without putting yourself in danger.

Ingestion of substances. Salvia divinorum, ayahuasca, and peyote are some of the herbs that are ingested by shamans to connect themselves with the spirit realms. Although these are potent trance-inducers, they can also be deadly. You don't need to take mind-altering drugs and plants to do what psychics do.

You will know that you're in a psychic level if:

- You are totally relaxed and you're almost on the verge of sleeping
- You become aware of visions, sounds, and other phantom sensations
- Your mental chatter is silent
- You can feel that you're in Alpha or Theta (you feel different)

You can stay longer in that state by not thinking too much and by simply accepting whatever you experience without actively resisting or questioning it. If you feel yourself slipping into Beta, do the relaxation exercises again (relaxing physically and mentally, counting downwards, visualizing your deepening awareness, affirming your intentions, etc.

Chapter 3:
Preparing Yourself for Psychic Functioning by Sharpening Your Senses

Psychic information that you receive will be translated to sensory impressions, even though it didn't pass through your eyes, ears, etc. It's because your brain is used to getting data in the form of images, sounds, feelings, smells, and tastes. It will convert received psychic energy/information into something that you're accustomed to, so that you can comprehend the information and do something about it. The problem is that we normally don't pay attention to the things we perceive even with our regular senses. That's why we can easily miss psychic signals just as much as we ignore faint scents and passing glimmers.

To strengthen your psychic senses, you must first strengthen your ordinary senses. This ensures that you become aware of what your psychic mind is picking up.

Sight

Sharpen your sense of sight by being more conscious of what you're seeing. Spend some time absorbing the sights before you. Discern every shape, color, and detail. Do the same at night with the lights out – try to pick up the visual characteristics of things that you barely see. Be aware of your peripheral vision instead of focusing only on what lies in front of your line of sight. Do all these with the intention of increasing your psychic awareness.

Sound

Develop your hearing by silencing your internal dialogue and redirecting your awareness into things within and outside you. Listen to the sound of your breath, the voices of the people around you, the distant traffic, etc. Try to imagine who or what is producing the sounds that you hear. Or, listen to a song where a lot of instruments are used, then pick them apart. Don't overanalyze sounds, but simply let them soak into your consciousness.

Touch

Get differently textured objects and run your fingertips over them. Don't allow your mind to wander as you do so. Feel sensations that normally escape your attention, such as the weight of your clothes upon your skin, the positions of your arms and legs, and so on.

Smell

Take a deep breath and detect everything that you can smell where you are. Try to distinguish the different scents that reach your nose and guess where they come from. Pay attention to the quality of the air – if you observe closely enough, you will notice that the weather and season affects how the air smells. Smell various substances – perfumes, flowers, food, condiments, and even offending items like trash and rotting material.

Taste

Focus on what you're eating. Savor its flavors and guess the spices and ingredients that are used in the meal. When you're drinking a beverage, sip gradually instead of gulping it down. Taste substances that you don't normally do, such as foreign spices or non-food (but non-toxic) materials (your own skin, leather, plastic, etc.)

In general, you can:

- Pay more attention to the stimuli around you

- Choose a particular stimulus and focus on its details

- Hone one sense (sight, sound, etc.) by tuning out other sensations (by blindfolding yourself or using earplugs, for example)

- Develop all or several senses together

The most important thing to do is to have the intention of sharpening your five senses in order to enhance your psychic sense. You can make an affirmation like "I am developing the sense of (sight/sound/smell/etc.) to strengthen and sensitize my psychic senses," or, "I am now becoming more sensory and psychically aware."

Chapter 4: Psychic Skill Training

The previous sense-sharpening exercises prepare you to do clairvoyance, clairaudience, clairsentience, clairolfaction, clairgustance, and other psychic feats. You only have to reach your psychic level to receive sensory impressions that have a psychic nature. Other than that, here are some exercises for you to try:

Clairvoyance

Using Zener cards. Zener cards are a set of cards with a different symbol on each card (circle, cross, wave pattern, star, and square). You can make your own Zener cards with a piece of thin cardboard and a marker. You can use other symbols aside from those mentioned above. Playing cards will also work for this purpose. To use cards for clairvoyance enhancement, attain your psychic level and guess a face-down card's symbol before flipping it over.

Viewing hidden objects. Get containers that all look the same and put different items within each. Switch their positions and make sure you don't remember what item is in what box. When you are satisfied with the arrangement, number the box from 1 to 5 (or up to whatever number of boxes you have). Then, focus on the things within each box. Write down or sketch what you see in your mind's eye in a piece of paper, along with your guess about what could be inside the box (receive as many impressions as you can before rationally deciding on what the item may be).

We'll tackle more ways of developing clairvoyance later.

Clairaudience

Listening to nature sounds. Like what was mentioned before, nature brings relaxation, which is conducive for psychic functioning. Be in a place with natural sounds (pouring rain, chirping birds, crashing waves, etc.) Amidst the white noise, try to pick up words and phrases – they may be the thoughts of beings (corporeal and non-corporeal) in the place or your subconscious mind's messages for you. Putting your ear next to a seashell will also do the trick.

Attempting to listen in on other people's conversations. When you're in a public place, try to discover what people are talking about even if you can't hear them talking. Don't use your logic with this. Just be open to any ideas that pop in your head.

Clairsentience

Guessing the texture and material of hidden objects. This is similar to the clairvoyance exercise (viewing hidden objects) but you concentrate on tactile sensations instead of appearances.

Clairolfaction

Using smells to get information about something. Write down the names of aromatic objects on separate strips of paper. Fold them to hide what you wrote. Put them in a bowl, mix them well, and label each one with a number. Get a blank sheet of paper and put numbers – you will write your impressions beside each number. Go to your psychic level, pick a piece, and wait for whatever smell will reach you. Do these with all the pieces of paper. Afterwards, check whether you've guessed correctly.

Clairgustance

Using tastes to get information about something. Do the exercise above but use distinctly flavored food as your subjects and intend to receive taste impressions.

Going Beyond Time (Precognition and Retrocognition)

Because psychic abilities don't adhere to natural laws, time is not a limitation for them. It means that your psychic awareness can access the past and the future.

To bring your psychic focus to a point of time aside from now, you can do one or more of the following:

- Say to yourself that you are visiting (date or time period).

- Imagine moving along a timeline and reaching your desired time.

- Focus on a date.

- Ask your spirit guides to take you there.

Knowing the past (retrocognition). You can go to a particular date that's important to your elderly relatives. Write down what you perceive (this may come in several senses) then form your guess about what happened to him/her during that time. Confirm what you get with your relative.

Knowing the future (precognition). Choose a future date or situation, record it, and then tune in to the impressions that form in your mind. List these down. When the day arrives, review what you've written and compare it with what actually happened.

Reading Objects (Psychometry)

Gaining information from objects. Ask a person to lend you some of his/her belongings such as a ring, a pendant, or a picture. Hold the item in your hand and clear your mind. After a few moments, you will see images and hear sounds that may be related to the object you're holding. Simply say them the way they are; if you think that you're not in Alpha or Theta anymore, or if you don't get anything, stop. Then, formulate a story that strings the psychic impressions together. Let the owner tell you whether you got it right or not.

Sensing the energy of a place. You don't need to hold an object with your hands to read it. You can go to a place and open your psychic senses to detect its energetic characteristics. Discuss your impressions with people who are familiar with the location to know how accurate you are.

Using Dreams for Psychic Development

Sleep includes the full range of brainwaves, thus it's possible to be psychic while sleeping. There are times when dreams contain prophesies or revelations of truth. You can use the dream state to do psychic activities such as divining the future, getting information, solving problems, rehearsing skills, talking to other people (dead or alive), sending healing to yourself and others, and more. To do this, you need to train yourself to achieve lucid dreaming.

There are many ways to achieve lucidity (awareness) during dreaming. One way is to keep track of your dreams. Upon waking up, write everything that you remember from your dream. Do this every day. After you've collected around 10 dreams or more, notice if there are recurrent themes. For example, you may often dream of flying, distorted things, or unusual situations. Tell yourself repeatedly that when you encounter the same things again (such as dead relatives or finding yourself in a strange place), you will immediately realize that you are dreaming. Before sleeping, remind yourself of your intention to lucid dream and your chosen dream signs. Your mental program will cause you to wake up in the middle of the dream. When you do so, you can proceed to do any psychic skill that you want. Just say or imagine what you intend to do. For example, "I am visiting my friend" or "I am discovering what career is best for me."

Telepathy Practice

You can connect with another person or animal by visualizing an energetic cord between the two of you. Keep your mind blank and wait for whatever you might receive. You can also ask a question (example: is this person single?) or focus on a subject (the person's current love interest, for example).

Reading thoughts. You can attempt to read the thoughts of strangers or have a partner to practice with. If you do have a partner, let him/her draw 5 symbols of his/her choice. Instruct him/her to focus on each one. Connect to this person and draw or write what comes in your mind. When you're done, tell him/her to focus on the next item until you've gone through the entire list. Check the results.

Influencing thoughts. Telepathy works both ways – receiving and sending. Sent thoughts are usually received at the subconscious level, but if the receiver is attuned to his/her subconscious, he/she will also become aware of it. Get a partner who will receive your thoughts. Send a symbol or an image to him/her then check whether he/she receives it. You can also try sending instructions for the person to move a certain way (ex. Scratch his/her nose). You can do this by visualizing the person doing the action or by imagining you're doing the action yourself and transferring the motions to him/her.

Empathy Practice

Empathy is similar to telepathy except you're dealing with emotions and not thoughts. Receive emotions by connecting to a person or an animal (through visualization or intention) and being open to whatever you may feel next. The emotions may be symbolic (colors or words, for example) or you may feel exactly what the person or animal is feeling. You can likewise influence the other to feel what you want by sending emotion-laden ideas or by feeling the emotion and projecting it.

Telekinesis

Telekinesis is a difficult psychic skill that requires intense concentration. Some people theorize that exerting force upon objects has something to do with the release of the potential energy stored within a person's cells. Others say that it has something to do with altering gravitational waves through the use of the person's electromagnetism, which is controlled by his/her mind. There are some things you can do to develop this ability.

By moving small objects. You can use a pinwheel, a floating magnet, or any small item such as a piece of foil or a cigarette. Connect with the item and imagine it moving into the desired direction. You must imagine every step of movement that it will undergo, just like constructing a film made up of a series of individual frames. Then, release your instruction with the intention of letting it happen to the object. You can also project energy streams from your hands and let them hit the item.

By influencing the roll of dice. Visualize the dice showing up the number you chose. Roll this up to 50 times. Record the numbers that show up – if your chosen number shows up more often than the others, then you may be using your telekinetic ability.

When you have achieved success with simple telekinetic tests, you can move on to moving larger and more complex items. Just make sure to replenish your energy by keeping yourself healthy and absorbing good energies around you (imagine absorbing them like a sponge).

Psychic Healing

You can experiment with healing energies by projecting healing energy and destructive energy on two identical potted plants (you don't need to do this if you feel sorry for the plants, though!). You can set the qualities of the energy by simply intending it to have healing or harmful energies, or by visualizing it to have certain colors and characteristics that you associate with health or decay. Otherwise, you can send healing to someone or something through:

Projecting energies. Reiki and pranic healing are examples of healing that make use of projected energy. The difference is that in Reiki, you tap into a divine source of healing while in pranic healing, you use your own energies.

Visualizing health. You can also heal by imagining the person or creature to be healthy or by visualizing the afflicted body part to improve.

Using tools. You can use special tools for healing a diseased body part or organ. Create tools using your imagination, such as a filter to remove impurities, a suction tool to remove blockages, and so on. Imagine the patient right before you and treat him/her using the tools.

Clairvoyance-Related Psychic Skills:

Seeing Auras

Viewing auras are best done in dimly lit environments. Gaze softly at the edges of a person and try to capture faint hues, outlines, and sparkles. You may see the aura with your physical eyes, or you may see them mentally. You can strengthen your eyes by gazing at a candle flame directly for 5 minutes then closing your eyes for 30 seconds. Afterwards, position yourself at a right angle from the flame. Do not move your body but look at the flame with only your eyes. Stare for 5 minutes then close your eyes for half a minute. Face the opposite direction and do the same with the other eye. Do this nightly if possible. This will sensitize the cells of your eyes.

Seeing the Invisible

Seeing the unseen requires sensitized eyes and a receptive mind. Have an unfocused gaze by letting the things you see become blurred. You might capture things that weren't there before. As with the aura, it's easier to use psychic sight when the lights are dimmed. Otherwise, close your eyes and mentally roam your surroundings.

Interacting with the Unseen

Interaction with spirit beings requires a lot of knowledge that is beyond the scope of this book. You need to know what beings are out there, their natures, how to interact with them, and how to protect yourself from psychic attacks and occult dangers. Be careful when you see a sentient being using your psychic senses – you need not interact with them every time. Things to learn are spirit communication, classification of spirits, and psychic self-defense, to name a few.

A basic psychic defense method is constructing a psychic shield. Visualize a bubble of potent energy surrounding and protecting you. You can use any material and shape for your shield – some use concrete spikes while others use golden light...the possibilities are endless. You can also give special instructions to your shield, such as to release toxic energies and let in positive energies. Remember to recharge this shield every 24 hours.

Crystal Gazing

Crystal gazing involves the use of a crystal to perceive the unknown. There are books that prescribe the meaning of the visions that are spotted in the crystal. For example, white smoke means good things while black smoke means bad things, ascending smoke translates to yes while descending smoke is no, cool colors (green, blue, violet) mean benefits while warm colors (red, orange, yellow) mean harm, visions appearing on the left side are real while those on the right side are symbolic, and so on.

You can consult these interpretations but you need not be limited by them. Let your intuition tell you what the visions mean (more on this in the last chapter). You don't need a crystal ball either. You can also use any item that you can gaze at, such as a bowl of water, a reflective surface, the smoke of incense, or even a blank sheet of paper. You may see it on the object itself or the images may be projected into your mind like a hologram.

Remote Viewing

To remote view, select a target then have the intention of viewing it. Record whatever sights, symbols, sounds, and sensations come to you. You may hear words – write them down because they might describe the thing or location you are viewing.

Divination

Tarot, I-Ching, and runes are some systems of divination. When you buy a Tarot deck, you will gain a manual that gives instructions and interpretations for the cards that are drawn. Rune sets may or may not have a book – anyway, you can buy rune books separately. The I-Ching is the book itself; there are books that explain how the I-Ching oracle is used, but the divinatory tools are yarrow sticks, 3 coins, or I-Ching cards. These systems of divination and others have their own set interpretation. However, you can deviate from these and make your own in accordance to your psychic impressions. For example, a Tarot card that is traditionally interpreted as 'achievement' may be read as 'opportunities from afar' because the appearance of incoming ships struck you. Go with your psychic insights; they are usually more accurate than book interpretations.

Seeing Visions

Visions can be seen on crystal balls, dreams, or hanging in mid-air. When you train both your mind's eye and your physical eyes with psychic sight, visions will come naturally to you.

Chapter 5:
Honing Your Clairvoyance and Other Psychic Abilities

To summarize:

- Psychic abilities are innate in every person

- Alpha and Theta brainwaves encourage psychic awareness and skills

- You can reach the psychic level by relaxing, among other methods

- Psychic abilities are trained by using them, checking for accuracy, analyzing the results, and modifying approaches according to the results

- You can gain psychic information by clearing your mind and asking a question, focusing on a subject, or being open to any information that may come through

- You can project energies by visualizing them

Aside from that, you need to accomplish the following:

Distinguish genuine psychic information from other things like imagination, fears, expectations, and projections

To receive psychic impressions accurately, you need to completely remove all expectations and concerns from your mind. These will influence what turns up in your awareness. If you know that this is impossible, at least be on the lookout for what's lurking in your subconscious and how they might change the data that you gather. The more that you practice relaxation and detachment, the better your ability in gaining non-biased results becomes.

Interpret psychic impressions

Your psychic level of mind does not function the same way as your ordinary mind, thus expect it to have a different language. You will need to make a psychic dictionary for this as the subconscious is fond of symbols and metaphors. You can do the following:

Ask your subconscious mind about its signals for certain words and ideas. For example, ask "What is my signal for joy?" You might see sunlight, feel warmth, or hear laughing children. Do these with other significant terms such as yes/no, alive/dead, health/illness, safety/danger, etc. List these responses down.

Sense energies and let them become converted into sensory impressions. If you want to know how 'anger' is perceived by your subconscious, attempt to sense it while anger is present (such as during a fight). Open your psychic senses – the energy might present itself as a bitter taste, a sound of banging drums, or a distorted face. Again, list these down. You can also sense the energy of your choice even by imagining them, recalling them from experience, or viewing their representations on pictures or paintings.

Review your psychic impressions. Compare your received impressions with your objective analysis. How do the impressions relate to the subject/results? Translating is a trial-

and-error process – don't worry about it; you will figure out the language of your subconscious as time goes by.

Make your psychic abilities work reliably

You make your psychic skills work reliably by *using them, evaluating what happened,* and *modifying your approach according to previous results.* List down the conditions that are related to your psychic functioning: the time of day you used it, the position of the sun and moon (some notice that these have an effect on psychic functioning – find out if this holds true for you), your health, emotions, concerns, state of mind, companions, environment, diet, and so on. Think about what helped you get precise results and what made you lose your focus. Strive to replicate favorable conditions as much as you can.

When you're making mistakes more than getting correct impressions, figure out what went wrong. Remedy them instead of getting stressed out – frustration and negative emotions increase Beta waves. Developing psychic abilities requires constant and patient practice. Just keep at it – our minds learn fast when we regularly teach it stuff. Soon enough, you will be able to use clairvoyance and other valuable psychic skills naturally.

Conclusion

Thank you again for downloading this book!

I hope this book was able to help you learn more about clairvoyance and psychic development!

The next step is to put this information to use, and begin using your clairvoyant and psychic skills from home!

Also don't forget to download my **FREE** report on the 7 Keys for Successful Meditation by following the link - http://bit.ly/1F91lfl

Finally, if you enjoyed this book, please take the time to share your thoughts and post a review on Amazon. It'd be greatly appreciated!

Thank you and good luck!

www.ingramcontent.com/pod-product-compliance
Lightning Source LLC
LaVergne TN
LVHW021744060526
838200LV00052B/3468